99
TO CUT, SEW ~~~~~~ ~~CK
YOUR ~~SCARF~~

Faith Blakeney, Justina Blakeney &
Ellen Schultz of Compai

POTTER
CRAFT

NEW YORK

Published in the United States by Potter Craft, an imprint of the Crown Publishing Group, a division of Random House, Inc., New York.
www.clarksonpotter.com
wwww.pottercraft.com

POTTER CRAFT and colophon is a registered trademark of Random House, Inc.

Library of Congress Cataloging-in-Publication Data is available

Printed in China

Graphic design by Compai

10 9 8 7 6 5 4 3 2 1

First Edition

contents

scarf sizes

small square: about 12" (30.5cm) x 12" (30.5cm)
medium square: from 13–24" (33cm–61cm) x 13–24" (33cm–61cm)
large square: from 25–35" (63.5–88.5cm) x 25–35" (63.8cm–88.5cm)
extra large square: 36" (91cm) x 36" (91cm) or larger
small rectangle: about 7" (18cm) wide x 12" (30.5cm) long
medium rectangle: from 8–16" (20.5cm–40.5cm) wide x 13–24" (33cm–61cm) l
large rectangle: from 17–24" (43cm–61cm) wide x 25–35" (63.5–88.5cm) long
extra large rectangle: from 25" (63.5cm) wide x 36" (91cm) long or larger
small oblong: about 3" (7.5cm) wide x 12" (30.5cm) long
medium oblong: from 4–8" (10cm–20.5cm) wide x 13–24" (33cm–61cm) long
large oblong: from 9–14" (23cm–35.5cm) wide x 25–35" (63.5–88.5cm) long
extra large oblong: from 15" (38cm) wide x 36" (91cm) long or longer

oreword

ra Neumann was one of the first designers to show women the
itless ways of wearing a scarf—her scarves have been sold in
er 20,000 stores worldwide and her style and sophistication has
en, and continues to be, a true inspiration. From Marilyn Monroe
Picasso to the girls of Compai, Vera Scarves has a long list of
al admirers.

ile everybody who knows anything about scarves knows Vera
d her colorful, handpainted designs, few know that, like Compai,
e began as a recycler. In the mid-1940s, Vera Neumann was
king art on everyday place mats. Soon World War II had begun,
d cotton and linen were scarce. What did Vera do? She used the
k from parachutes—and a scarf business was born!

99 Ways to Cut, Sew, Tie & Rock Your Scarf, Compai shows you
amazing ways to style that fabulous fashion accessory into a
arable work of art!

san Seid
esident
e VERA® Company

introduction

This is not just any book. This is the third (yeah you heard us! we said third!) installment in a series of books that constitutes a new movement in fashion. Ours is a little company with a big vision. We are three best friends trying to make a difference. We aim to infuse fashion with new meaning—to rehabilitate it—using existing materials to create new fashion trends. This series is a way to share our know-how with you. First we showed you how to **transform your t-shirt** in *99 Ways to Cut, Trim, & Tie Your T-Shirt into Something Special,* but you wanted more, so we taught you how **deck out your denim** in *99 Ways to Cut, Sew, & Deck Out Your Denim*. Now, our fine fashionista friends, we proudly present to you . . . *99 Ways to Cut, Sew, Tie, & Rock Your Scarf*. We, COMPAI, the clothes recycling mavens, have hooked up with VERA, the dopest scarf company on the planet, to guide you on the path of style enlightenment. So fasten your seat belts, open your minds, and get ready for COMPAI's most colorful journey yet. Grab your old scarves and get to cuttin'!

ATTENTION!!!

'ore embarking on this adventure, there are a few things to keep in
ND, HEART, and SPIRIT. Most importantly, free your mind! We're all
ists. Choose projects wisely. Be sure that DIMENSIONS and
ATERIALS are right, I.E. don't make a shopping tote from a fine silk
rf. Take into consideration the qualities of your SCARF (DURABILITY,
LOR, PATTERN, TRANSPARENCY), and use them to your advantage!
w with care and caution. Read through the instructions and the
responding technical drawings before beginning each project. It's
ential to understand each step to calculate dimensions and ensure
per fit. The **bold-faced** words are references to the glossary of
hniques in the back of the book. It's a PRICELESS TREASURE of
ving lessons and vocab. USE IT, and use it wisely. Remember to recycle
D STUFF. Ask your gramma for her old scarves (preferably VERA!) or
d them at your local thrift store. If there's a project that requires
stic, cut it off an old pair of panties. You laugh, but we're serious! It's
nomical and ecological. Our estimates for quantity of fabric, elastic,
. are just that—estimates. We tried to err on the side of excess, but
t doesn't mean that you should. Whenever you can, use scarf scraps
tead of entire scarves. Often projects require ribbons, why not make
bons from a scrap? Waste not want not.

me estimates are based on the use of a sewing machine
ars signify level of difficulty *=easy; ****=difficult
eam allowance = .5 inches unless otherwise noted
emember measurements will vary according to your size.

1

grace

kelly-style scarf

You'll need
1 small square scarf

1. fold scarf in half on the diagonal
2. drape scarf over your head and wrap around your neck, crossing in front (as shown)
3. tie a **simple knot** in back

#2
sirena
babydoll top

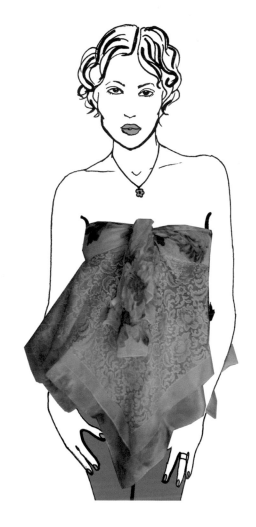

You'll need

1 medium square scarf (a)

1 large square scarf (b)

1 large oblong scarf (c)

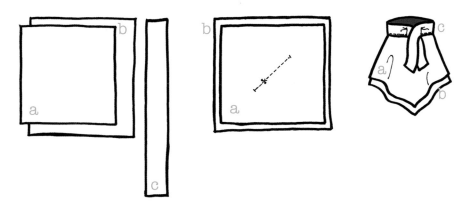

1. cut a diagonal slit slightly larger than the circumference of your bust in the center of scarves (a) and (b)
2. keeping scarves (a) and (b) lined up, **clean finish sew** scarf (c) around slits of scarves (a) and (b)— be sure scarf (c) dangles evenly on both ends to be tied at bust
3. slip on your new top and tie (c) in front

#3

phyllis
long-sleeved top

You'll need

1 large rectangular scarf (a)

2 medium square scarves (b) and (c)

1 long-sleeved shirt

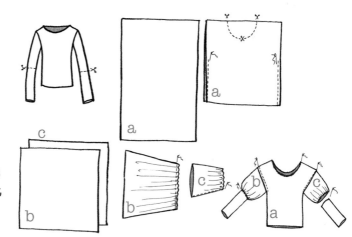

1. cut sleeves off shirt at elbows
2. fold scarf (a) in half widthwise
3. cut u-neck from folded edge
4. **clean finish sew** halfway up sides of (a) [ATTN: the part you leave unsewn will be the armholes, so make sure they are the same length as half of scarves (b) and (c)]
5. **gather** 1 side of scarves (b) and (c)
6. **clean finish sew** scarves (b) and (c) into tube shapes as shown
7. **clean finish sew** (b) and (c) onto (a) at armholes
8. **clean finish sew** shirt sleeves onto gathered edges of (b) and (c)

#4

sasha
butterfly top

You'll need

2 medium rectangular scarves

(a) and (b)

1 large oblong scarf (c)

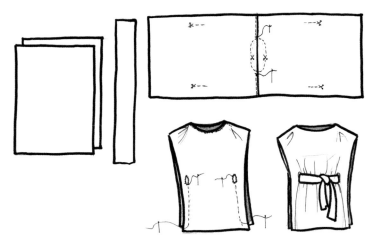

1. place (a) and (b) together with 2 short edges
2. mark an oval in the center (large enough for your head to fit through)
3. cut out head hole as marked, and **zigzag stitch** around raw edge
4. **clean finish sew** both scarves together at shoulders
5. cut 2 slits in each scarf for belt loops
6. **zigzag stitch** around belt loops
7. sew back and front together with stitches going from belt loops down to bottom edge of scarf, on both sides and thread scarf (c) through belt loops

avery

simple neck
wrap

You'll need

1 oblong scarf (of any size)

1. fold scarf in half lengthwise
2. place around your neck
3. pull scarf ends through fold as shown
4. did you know it could be so easy to do it euro style?

#6

allondra
simple halter

You'll need

1 large square scarf

0 sewing skills

1. take 2 parallel corners of scarf and tie around your neck using a **simple knot** creating a halter
2. tie 2 remaining corners around your waist in back using a **simple knot**
3. can you believe it's so easy to look so good?

#7

mia
bikini top

You'll need
1 large oblong scarf
(make sure it's wide
enough to cover your bust)
1 ribbon 36 inches (91.5 cm)

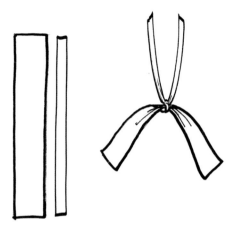

1. tie ribbon around the center of scarf making a **simple knot** as shown
2. tie scarf around your bust, making a **simple knot** in back
3. tie ribbon in a **simple knot** behind your neck

#8

rumi
sundress

You'll need
1 extra large square scarf
1 large oblong scarf
elastic strip (2 feet [61cm] long)

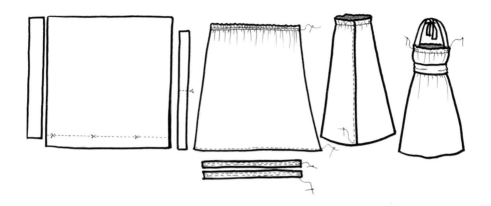

1. cut off a 3-inch (7.5cm) wide strip from 1 side of square scarf
2. cut strip in half widthwise
3. **flat hem** around the edges of both strips
4. sew elastic strip onto 1 side of square scarf (1 inch from edge) using **gathering with elastic** technique
5. **flat hem** raw edge of square scarf
6. **clean finish sew** unsewn edges of square scarf together to form dress
7. **clean finish sew** 2 strips onto dress for halter
8. tie in a simple knot at back of neck as shown

#9

makayla
twisted halter

You'll need
1 large square scarf
0 sewing skills

inside out view

pinch knot

1. tie a small **pinch knot** in the center of scarf
2. with the knot facing you, tie top corners together around neck using a **simple knot**
3. tie bottom corners together around waist using a **simple knot**

#10

eley

bracelet

You'll need
1 scarf any size

1. cut 2 strips lengthwise; cut one 3 inches (7.5cm) wide and the other 2 inches (5cm) wide
2. sew both into 2 long tubes using **tube** technique
3. cut remainders of scarf into small pieces for stuffing [ATTN: to make a necklace, you will need additional strips]
4. stuff long tubes with pieces of remaining scarf
5. cut long tubes into 3-inch (7.5cm) long pieces
6. make a ring from the 2-inch (5cm) wide piece, sew it shut
7. link a wide tube to the ring and sew it closed
8. continue this process of alternating from 1 width tube to the other to make a chain
9. when chain is long enough to fit your arm (or neck), link ends together

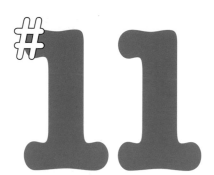

11

kendra

tunic

You'll need
1 extra-large square scarf (a)
1 small square scarf (b)

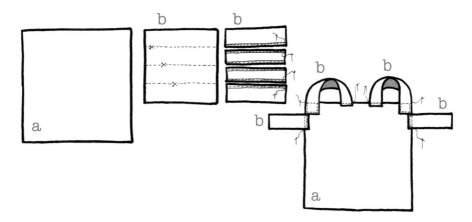

1. cut scarf (b) into 4 equal strips
2. **flat hem** the raw sides of each strip
3. sew 1 end of a strip onto top left corner of the front of scarf (a), as shown; repeat on right side
4. top stitch around the strips in a square for reinforcement
5. wrap scarf (a) around your body with 2 attached strips in front and then **top stitch** unsewn ends to the back creating 2 shoulder straps as indicated
7. **top stitch** the 2 remaining strips to scarf (a) just below shoulder straps in front where indicated, and tie in a bow

laila

knotted halter

You'll need
1 large square scarf

1. cut 3 2-inch (5cm) wide strips from one side of scarf
2. cut 1 strip in half widthwise and tie each short strip onto a bottom corner with a **simple knot**
3. **plain knot** the other 2 corners as shown
4. tie 2 **simple knots** in the center of 1 strip as shown
5. attach knotted strip to 2 top corners with **simple knots**
6. attach last strip to knotted strip with 2 **simple knots**
7. tie in back around waist

#13

robin
muu-muu

You'll need
2 extra-large rectangular scarves
(a) and (b)
2 extra-large square scarves (c) and (d)
[we suggest using transparent scarves]

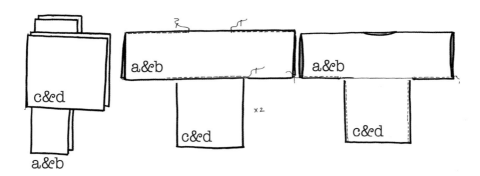

1. place scarves (a) and (b) on top of each other
2. **clean finish sew** top edges of (a) and (b) together BUT leave at least a 1 foot (30.5cm) hole in the center for your head opening
3. **clean finish sew** (c) onto (a) in center as shown
4. **clean finish sew** (b) onto (d) in center as shown
5. **clean finish sew** sides and sleeves closed where indicated (don't worry if they are not exactly the same length, as in photo, that's part of the look!)
6. smile because you have just created one of the sexiest muu-muus of the season!

#14

luella

covered buttons

You'll need
1 small scarf
1 jacket with ugly buttons
(buttons should be at least the size of a nickel)

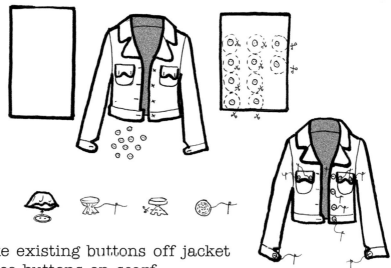

1. take existing buttons off jacket
2. place buttons on scarf
3. cut out circles that measure 1 inch (2.5cm) larger (in circumference) than the buttons
4. place 1 scarf circle over the top of a button
5. pinch fabric together underneath button and sew, keeping scarf circle taut
6. cut off excess material under button
7. repeat with all buttons
8. **sew buttons** back onto the jacket (use many stitches to make sure that your new, precious buttons are secure!)

15

soledad

boho head wrap

You'll need
1 large square scarf

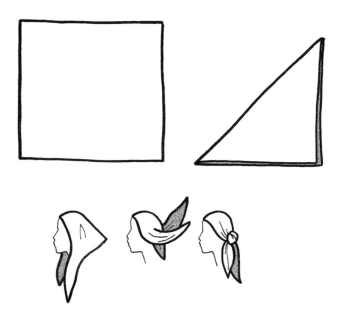

1. fold scarf in half on the diagonal
2. place on your head with 2 scarf ends hanging equally on either side of face
3. tie ends into a **simple knot** in back of your head, tucking in triangular piece underneath the knot

#16

sabine
shorts

You'll need
1 large oblong scarf
(long enough to wrap around waist and tie)
1 extra-large square scarf

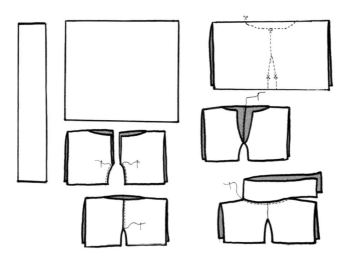

1. fold square scarf in half
2. cut a slit in fold slightly larger than the circumferance of your hips
3. cut scarf in half using **pattern technique** to create crotch. [ATTN: back and front are different]
4. keeping pieces folded, **clean finish sew** front and back crotch and inside leg seams
5. **clean finish sew** oblong scarf around slit of shorts making sure that the leftover lengths of the scarf hang down equally on one side
6. slip your shorts on and tie waistband

17

joni
necklace

You'll need
1 medium oblong scarf
6 plastic bottle caps

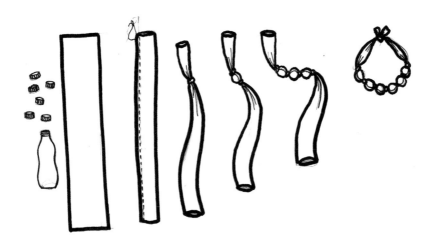

1. fold scarf in half lengthwise and sew into tube using **tube technique**
2. tie **plain knot** in tube several inches/cm from one end; insert bottle cap into tube, and tie another **plain knot**
3. repeat process until all bottle caps are in tube and all knots are tied
4. tie around your neck—you're a star!

#18

ellen

kahlo style hairdo

You'll need

1 large oblong scarf

1 head of long hair

1. part your hair down the middle
2. place scarf around your neck with ends
   hanging in front
3. braid scarf into your hair on each side
   using scarf as third strand in each braid
4. tie the scarf ends in a **simple knot** on
   the top of your head

#19

madeline
winter vest

You'll need
1 extra-large oblong wool scarf

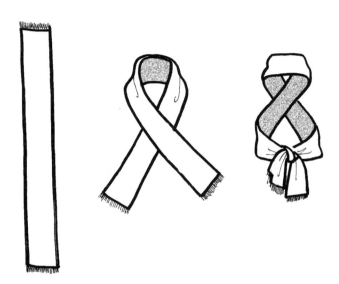

1. place scarf around your neck
2. cross over chest as shown
3. tie a **simple knot** in back

#20
shannon
v-neck tank

#21
milly
loose halter

You'll need
1 large rectangular scarf
1 large oblong scarf

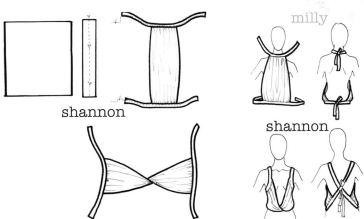

shannon

milly

shannon

[ATTN: projects 20–23 use the same pattern, sew 1 pattern, and wear it 4 different ways!]

1. cut oblong scarf in half lengthwise
2. center rectangular scarf between 2 strips as shown and sew strips onto rectangular scarf using **gathering** technique
3. FOR SHANNON: lay out piece with strips on side; twist as shown
4. lay strips over shoulders with twist in front join all 4 strips together and tie in back as shown
3. FOR MILLY: drape 2 straps over shoulders and tie around neck in back
4. tie bottom strips in back

#22

klara
strapless top

#23

anna
asymmetrical top

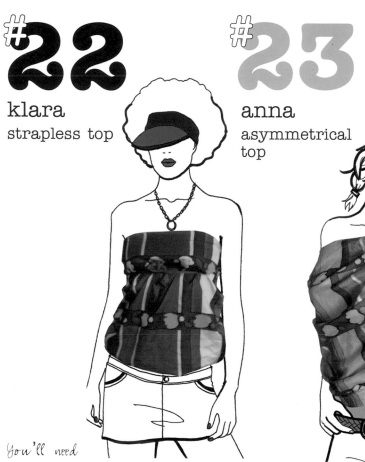

You'll need

1 large rectangular scarf

1 large oblong scarf

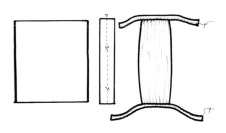

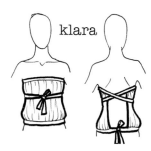

klara

anna

[ATTN: projects 20–23
use the same pattern,
sew 1 pattern, and wear
it 4 different ways!]

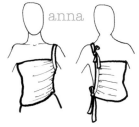

1. cut oblong scarf in half
   lengthwise
2. center rectangular scarf between 2 strips as
   shown and sew strips onto rectangular scarf
   using **gathering** technique
3. FOR KLARA: wrap around torso with all strips
   in back
4. cross top strips in back and tie under bust in front
5. tie bottom strips in back as shown
3. FOR ANNA: wrap around torso so that straps are
   hanging at shoulders and at waist; tie straps in
   simple knots

24

winter

handkerchief skirt

You'll need
1 large square scarf
1 large oblong scarf

1. cut diagonal slit in center of square scarf slightly larger than the circumference of your waist
2. carefully slip it on to ensure a good fit on hips
3. **clean finish sew** oblong scarf around slits making sure the ends are even on both sides [ATTN: leave 2 inches (5cm) of skirt unattached to oblong scarf to allow for tying—it will make life easier]
4. slip on your skirt and tie waistband on the side

#25

virginia
bow tank top

You'll need
1 tank top or t-shirt
1 large oblong scarf

1. tie oblong scarf into a bow (the bow should be about the same width as the width of your top)
2. fasten bow to top by **hand stitching** each corner and center of your bow to top as shown
3. that's it. Can you believe it? You're a genius!

#26

kelsey
beach cover-up

You'll need
1 extra-large scarf
2 vintage buttons

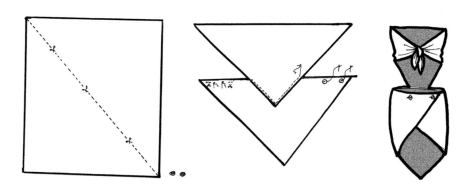

1. cut scarf in half on the diagonal
2. **pin** bottom corner of 1 piece onto other as shown
3. try on to ensure good fit
4. **top stitch** bottom corner of 1 piece to other
   as shown
5. make 2 **buttonholes** on 1 side of bottom scarf
   where indicated
6. on the opposite side of bottom scarf sew on
   2 buttons
7. that's it girl—you're ready for Brazil!

#27

susan
party dress

#28

terry
skirt with suspenders

You'll need

1 large square scarf

1 large oblong scarf

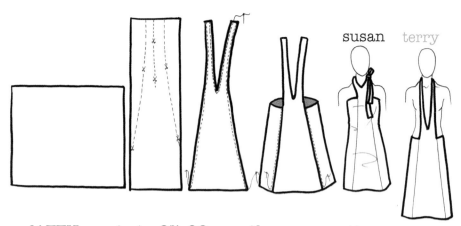

[ATTN: projects 27–28 use the same pattern, sew 1 pattern and wear it 2 different ways!]

2. cut slit lengthwise in center of oblong scarf (about ⅓ of total length of scarf)
3. Cut sides off of oblong scarf lengthwise as shown
4. **flat hem** raw edges
5. **clean finish sew** square scarf to bottom of oblong scarf creating a **tube**
6. FOR SUSAN: slip on as a dress and tie strips in back of neck as a halter
6. FOR TERRY: slip on as a skirt and tie in back as a halter

#29

shay
purse with rings

You'll need

1 medium rectangular scarf

1-liter plastic water bottle

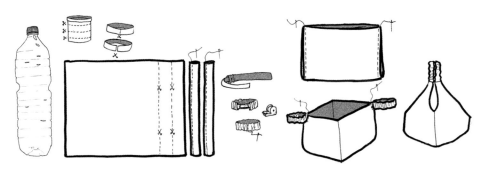

1. cut two 2 inch (5cm) wide strips from scarf on short end
2. sew 2 strips into 2 tubes using **tube** technique
3. cut container across creating 2 rings, cut them open as shown
4. push plastic strips through each tube using **threading through** technique
5. tape ends of plastic strips together to re-create ring
6. sew tubes closed
7. fold scarf in half and **clean finish sew** up sides
8. **hand stitch** rings onto each side of bag, reinforcing with many stitches

#30

francis
knot necklace

You'll need
1 medium oblong scarf
cotton for stuffing
1 chain (2.5 feet [76cm] long)
3 metal jump rings (2 large ones and 1 small one)

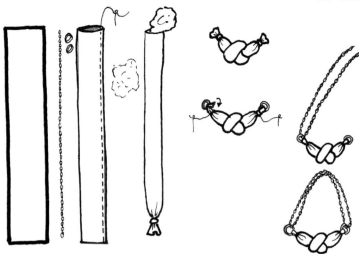

1. fold scarf in half lengthwise
2. sew into tube using **tube** technique
3. tie small **plain knot** on 1 end and stuff the tube with cotton like a sausage!
4. make a big **plain knot** in the middle of your sausage and another small **plain knot** on the end
5. pass knotted ends through the metal jump rings and secure them with a few stitches
6. thread chain through both sides of metal rings as shown and join them together with the small jump ring

#31
jolene
kimono-style top

You'll need

1 extra-large rectangular scarf (a)

1 large square scarf (b)

1 ribbon about 10 (3m) ft long

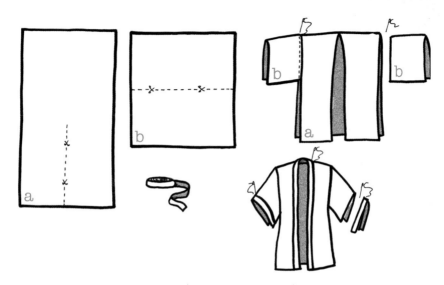

1. cut a lengthwise slit halfway up the center of scarf (a)
2. cut square scarf (b) in half
3. fold scarf (a) in half with slit in front
4. **clean finish sew** the two halves of scarf (b) onto either side of scarf (a) as open sleeves as shown
5. cut ribbon into three pieces; 1 long for extended collar trim, and 2 short for sleeve trim
6. sew ribbon onto sleeves and collar using **border** technique

32

willow

party purse

You'll need
1 large oblong scarf
1 small square scarf
2 vintage buttons

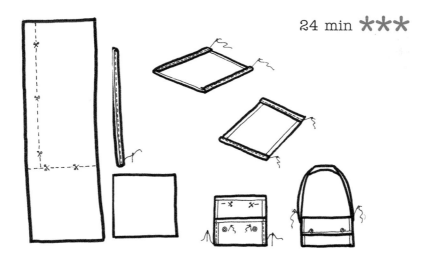

24 min ★★★

1. cut a square piece out of oblong scarf that is 1½ inches (3.8cm) larger than square scarf on all sides
2. cut 3-inch (7.5cm) wide strip from remaining oblong scarf for shoulder strap and then **flat hem**
3. placing square scarf on top of larger square piece, fold over 2 opposite edges of larger square piece and stitch using **border** technique
4. fold and stitch the two remaining edges using **border** technique
5. fold square to create "envelope" as shown
6. **top stitch** short sides of envelope closed
7. make 2 **buttonholes** in flap and sew on **buttons**
8. **top stitch** strap onto sides of your stunning new bag!

#33

trina

poolside top

You'll need
1 large square scarf

 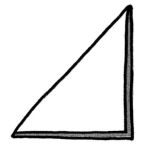 

1. fold scarf in half on the diagonal
2. tie 2 corners together in front using a **simple knot**

#34

rose
flower hair band

You'll need
1 medium oblong scarf
(long enough to wrap around your head and tie)

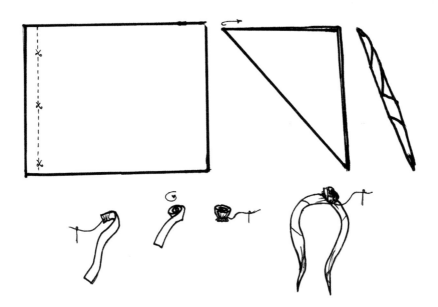

1. cut 1½ (3.8cm) inch strip from 1 edge of scarf
2. fold scarf in half on diagonal
3. **roll** up scarf
4. sew strip into a flower by **gathering**, **rolling**, and **hand stitching**, as shown
5. **stitch** flower securely onto rolled scarf
6. tie ends of scarf in a **simple knot** in back of your head

#35

erin

balloon skirt

You'll need

1 extra-large rectangular scarf (a)

1 large oblong scarf (b)

(long enough to wrap around your waist and tie)

1. fold scarf (a) in half lengthwise
2. **gather** scarf (a) while sewing it to the center of the oblong scarf (b) [ATTN: the length of gathered scarf (a) must be 2 inches longer than the circumference of your hips]
3. **clean finish sew** double sides of (a) together to close skirt leaving 3 inches (7.5cm) open at the top near the waistband
4. tie waistband in a bow at hip

#36
farrah
daytime bag

You'll need
1 large oblong scarf
1 large square scarf

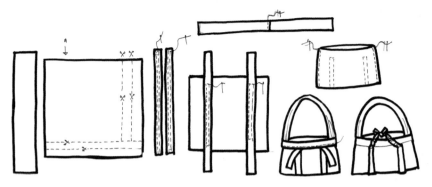

1. cut 2 2½ inch (6.5cm) strips from 1 side of square scarf
2. **flat hem** raw edges
3. cut 2 2½ inch (6.5cm) strips from perpendicular side of scarf
4. **clean finish sew** shorter strips together creating 1 long strip
5. **top stitch** longer strips across square scarf so that they are parallel for reinforcement—be sure to leave 1 inch (2.5cm) on each end unsewn
6. fold in half to form envelope shape and **clean finish sew** sides
7. use **border** technique to sew long strip to edge of bag opening and to attach oblong scarf for shoulder strap
8. tie reinforcing strips together to close bag

#37

gwen
hairband

You'll need
1 medium oblong scarf
1 plastic headband

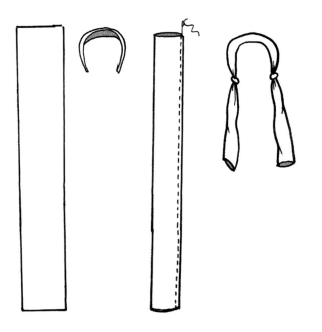

1. measure headband width at widest point
2. fold scarf in half lengthwise and cut to ½ inch (13mm) wider than twice headband width—be sure to cut on open side, not fold
3. sew into **tube**
4. slip headband into tube and center it
5. tie **plain knots** at both ends of the headband to secure in place

#38

adena
summer halter

You'll need
1 large rectangular scarf
1 medium oblong scarf

1. fold over 1½ inches (3.8cm) of the shorter edge of rectangular scarf and **top stitch** to create a hem
2. **thread** oblong scarf **through** hem
3. tie long scarf around neck
4. tie bottom corners together in back

#39

johanna
bikini bottom

You'll need
1 medium square scarf

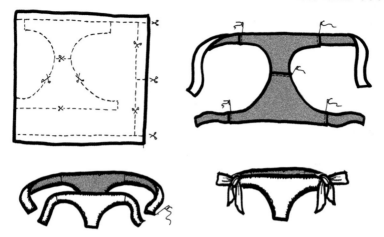

1. cut off 2 1½ inches (3.8cm) wide strips, from parallel sides of scarf
2. cut off a strip 1½ inches (3.8cm) wide, from 1 of the remaining sides of scarf
3. cut that strip in half widthwise
4. cut out form indicated in illustration using **pattern** technique
5. **clean finish sew** short strips onto front of bikini
6. **clean finish sew** longer strips onto back of bikini
7. **zigzag** stitch all raw edges for a clean finish, slip it on, and tie sides together in a **simple knot**
8. now flip to #7 Mia and make the top, girl!

#40

jen

handkerchief top

You'll need
1 large square scarf
1 large oblong scarf

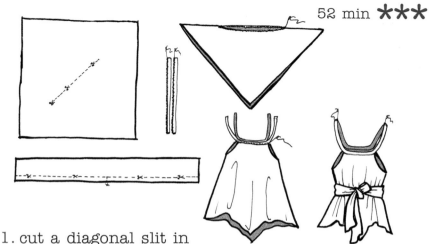

52 min ★★★

1. cut a diagonal slit in the center of square scarf (make sure that it is big enough to fit around your bust)
2. cut a strip lengthwise from oblong scarf that is 1 inch (2.5cm) wide
3. cut strip in half lengthwise
4. **zigzag** stitch around slit in square scarf
5. sew strip onto front of slit in the center as shown (be sure to leave space for armholes)
6. repeat with other strip in back
7. sew strips together, as shown, creating shoulder straps
8. use leftover strip of oblong scarf as belt and tie in a bow

#41

nikki

lantern
cover

You'll need
1 large square scarf
1 paper lantern

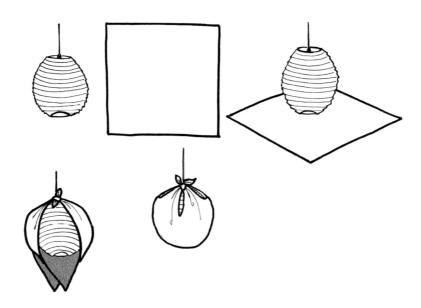

1. place lantern in center of scarf
2. tie 2 diagonal corners on top of lantern near hanging cord with a **simple knot**
3. tie remaining diagonal corners upwards and tie together with existing **simple knot**
4. hang lantern and enjoy the glow!

#42

caramia

racer back top

You'll need
1 large square scarf

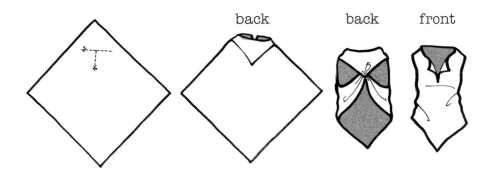

back   back   front

1. place scarf on the diagonal and cut 1 horizontal slit 6 inches (15cm) long in upper corner [ATTN: leave at least 3 inches (7.5cm) on either side of slit intact]
2. cut a vertical slit downwards from center of existing slit, 6 inches (15cm) long
3. fold small triangle above horizontal slit back and down
4. join folded down corner with 2 side corners and **top stitch** closed as shown

#43

justina
sporty bag

You'll need

2 medium rectangular scarves

(a more durable material is recommended—cotton, linen, synthetic)

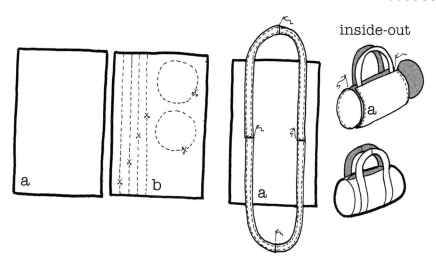

inside-out

1. cut 4 strips 1½ inches (3.8cm) long lengthwise from scarf (b) and **flat hem**
2. cut 2 circular pieces out of scarf (b) making sure the circumference is equal to the length of the long side of scarf (a)
4. **clean finish sew** 4 strips together at each end, creating 1 long oval band
5. **top stitch** long oval band onto scarf (a) as shown, leaving 2 ends of the oval for straps
6. **clean finish sew** circular pieces from scarf (b) onto the sides of scarf (a)—now work it!

44

noalena
baby bib

You'll need

1 small square scarf

2 sheets of pvc plastic

(12 inches x 12 inches/30.5 cm x 30.5 cm)

hole punch (the stronger the better)

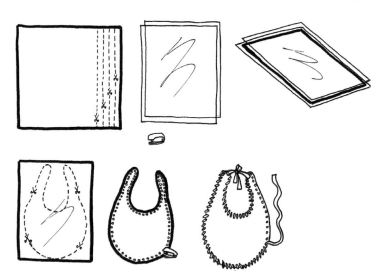

1. cut 4 ½-inch (13mm) wide strips from scarf
2. place remaining scarf between 2 sheets of pvc
3. cut out desired bib shape
4. hole punch around bib shape
5. sew 3 strips end to end into 1 long strip
6. lace strip through holes, securing each piece in place all around edge
7. cut the remaining strip in half
8. tie halves to holes at either side of bib opening and fasten on your little one with a bow

#45

rebecca

summer dress

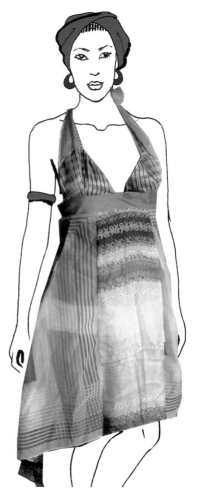

You'll need

2 large square scarves (a), (b)

1 medium square scarf (c)

1 large oblong scarf (d)

1 vintage button

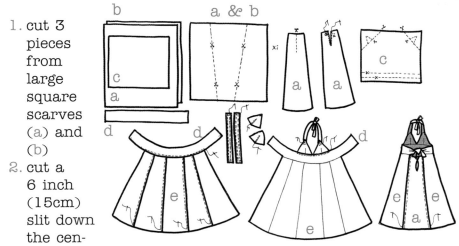

1. cut 3 pieces from large square scarves (a) and (b)

2. cut a 6 inch (15cm) slit down the central piece from scarf (a) as indicated, **flat hem** raw edges of slit, make **buttonhole**, sew on **button**

3. cut 2 2-inch (5cm) wide strips from longer side of scarf (c) and **flat hem**

4. cut off corners of scarf (c) [ATTN: corners need to cover your breasts] create **closed darts**

6. **clean finish sew** 5 remaining pieces from (a) and (b) long sides together, shortest edges upwards creating (e)

7. **clean finish sew** short side of (e), center it on (d)

8. **pin and sew** triangles into place on the oblong scarf (d)

9. sew strips from (c) onto corners of triangles for straps

10. **clean finish sew** piece (a) together with (e) in back

11. tie scarf (d) and halter neck straps in back. YAY!

#46

faith

neck bow

You'll need

1 medium rectangular scarf

1. drape scarf around neck
2. tie into bow
3. now smile—you look sooo cute!

47

amanda

knotted belt

You'll need
3 large oblong scarves
(the wider the scarf the thicker your belt will be)

1. lay scarves on top of each other, loop at one end, and secure together with **plain knot**
2. braid down a few inches and make another **plain knot**; repeat until 6 inches (15cm) from end
3. thread scarf ends through loop and tie a **simple knot** to secure

#48

amira

party dress
with knots

You'll need

4 medium square scarves (a, b, c, and d)

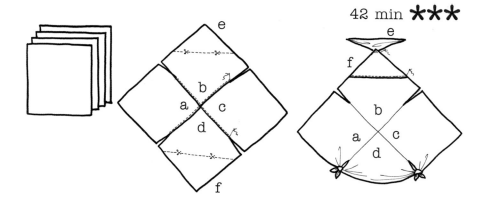

1. place scarves (a, b, c, and d) together creating a large square as shown; and pin in place
2. sew a large X in the middle of the 4 scarves to connect them, but leave open slits at the ends
3. cut off corners of (b) and (d) to create pieces (e) and (f)
4. **clean finish sew** piece (f) onto raw edge of scarf (b)
5. sew piece (e) onto piece (f), corner to corner
6. **simple knot** 2 bottom slits, as shown
7. **clean finish sew** backsides of pieces (a) and (c) together, and tie with a **simple knot** at the top
8. tie together corners of piece (b) with a **simple knot**

#49

milo
pillowcase

You'll need

2 medium square scarves

2 vintage buttons

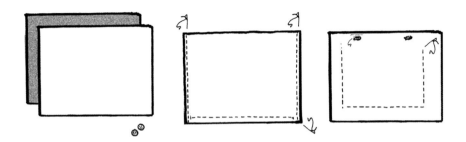

1. place scarves on top of each other
2. **clean finish sew** 3 edges of scarves as shown
3. **top stitch** around same 3 edges leaving 1½ inches (3.8cm) from edge intact
4. make **buttonholes** and sew **buttons** in center of opening
5. slip your pillow into the case; sweet dreams!

#50

bianca
party gown

You'll need

1 extra-large rectangular scarf

2 large oblong scarves

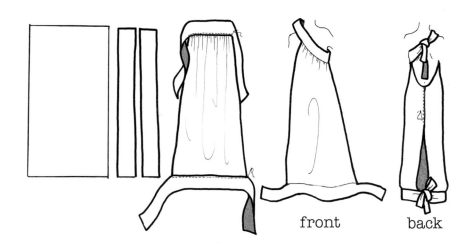

front   back

[ATTN: projects 50–54 use the same pattern
1. center rectangular scarf between 2 oblong scarves
2. **clean finish sew** 1 oblong scarf onto rectangular scarf
3. **clean finish sew** other oblong scarf onto rectangular scarf using **gathering** technique
4. place gathered end over 1 shoulder and under the other arm as shown; tie in back
5. **clean finish sew** back together creating a deep-cut back, leaving a slit open toward the bottom
6. tie bottom end in bow in back

51

jasmine

party top

You'll need

1 extra-large rectangular scarf

2 large oblong scarves

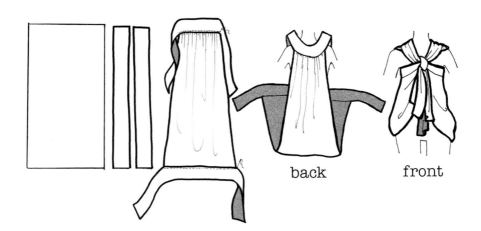

back

front

[ATTN: projects 50–54 use the same pattern

1. center rectangular scarf between 2 oblong scarves
2. **clean finish sew** 1 oblong scarf onto rectangular scarf
3. **clean finish sew** other oblong scarf onto rectangular scarf using **gathering** technique
4. drape gathered end over shoulders as shown
5. fold the other end underneath and upward to armpits; then bring it around toward front, joining all ends by tying them together in front

#52

ophelia
strapless dress

You'll need

1 extra-large rectangular scarf

2 large oblong scarves

back

[ATTN: projects 50–54 use the same pattern

1. center rectangular scarf between 2 oblong scarves
2. **clean finish sew** 1 oblong scarf onto rectangular scarf
3. **clean finish sew** other oblong scarf onto rectangular scarf using **gathering** technique
4. tie gathered end around your waist in back making sure the fabric is inside-out
5. **clean finish sew** long edges together from tied waist downward to cover your bum
6. bring bottom end up over your bust and under your arms; tie in back

#53

fey

disco dress

You'll need

1 extra-large rectangular scarf

2 large oblong scarves

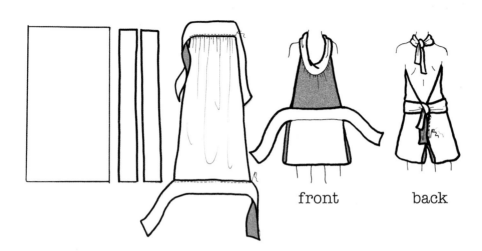

front   back

[ATTN: projects 50–54 use the same pattern
1. center rectangular scarf between 2 oblong scarves
2. **clean finish sew** 1 oblong scarf onto rectangular scarf
3. **clean finish sew** other oblong scarf onto rectangular scarf using **gathering** technique
4. tie gathered end loosely around neck in back with fabric hanging inside-out in front
5. bring other end up to waist and tie in back
6. **clean finish sew** long edges together from tied waist downward to cover your bum

#54

jocelyn

harem-style shorts

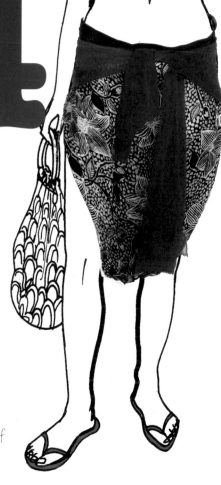

You'll need

1 extra-large rectangular scarf

2 large oblong scarves

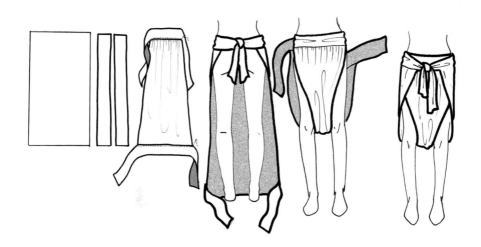

[ATTN: projects 50–54 use the same pattern
1. center rectangular scarf between 2 oblong scarves
2. **clean finish sew** 1 oblong scarf onto rectangular scarf
3. **clean finish sew** other oblong scarf onto rectangular scarf using **gathering technique**
4. tie gathered end around your waist in back
5. bring bottom end between your legs up to waist and tie in front as shown

#55

andrea
baby carrier

You'll need

1 large oblong cotton scarf

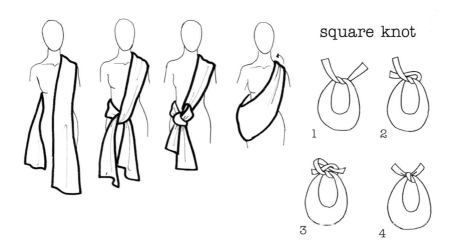

square knot

1   2   3   4

1. place scarf over 1 shoulder
2. tie **square knot** on opposite hip
3. rotate scarf so that knot is on your upper back
4. carefully place your tiny one in the baby carrier and go for a stroll [ATTN: be sure to secure knot! wear at your own risk]

56

selma

tunic dress

You'll need

2 large square scarves (a), (b)

(1 scarf must be long enough to

fit comfortably around waist)

1 medium square scarf (c)

5 vintage buttons

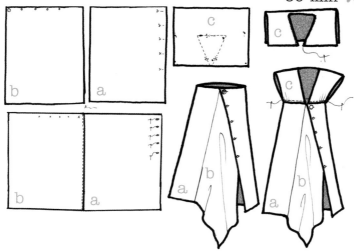

1. make 5 **buttonholes** on 1 side of scarf (a) as shown
2. sew 5 corresponding **buttons** onto scarf (b)
3. cut triangle from scarf (c) as shown (make sure your head can comfortably fit through) **zigzag stitch** around raw edge
4. **clean finish sew** scarves (a) and (b) together on 1 edge (make sure buttons and buttonholes are oriented as in illustration); bring scarf (b) around to scarf (a) and button
5. **clean finish sew** scarf (c) to (a) and (b) in front and back as shown (gather in front at bust if necessary)

#57

may
tank dress

You'll need

1 large square scarf

1 1-inch (2.5cm) wide ribbon 3 ft (1m) long

1 tank top

1. fold square scarf in half on the diagonal and cut into 2 triangles
2. cut triangle from front and back of tank top as shown
3. place scarf triangles into triangles cut from tank top and **clean finish sew** 1 to back and the other to front
4. **clean finish sew** up sides of scarf to create "skirt"
5. wrap ribbon around your waist—tie as you please!

58

noemi
satchel

You'll need
1 large square scarf
1 medium oblong scarf

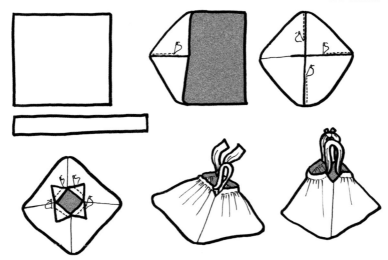

1. place scarf right side up and fold corners to center, like an envelope
2. **stitch** touching edges together, leaving about a 5 inch (12.5cm) squared opening where the corners meet
3. fold down little triangle corners, then sew as shown to create 4 1-inch (2.5cm) wide hems
4. flip bag inside-out
5. **thread** oblong scarf through hems, tie in a **simple knot**
6. pull on oblong scarf to create handles as shown

#59

anita

boxer shorts

You'll need

1 large rectangular scarf
1 ribbon 1 foot (30.5m) longer
than your waist

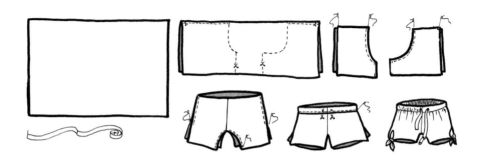

1. fold scarf in half lengthwise
2. use **pattern** technique to cut out 2 front and 2 back pieces of shorts [ATTN: back pieces and front pieces are different]
3. keeping front and back pieces aligned, **clean finish sew** crotch (leave small, straight edge unsewn)
4. lay out front and back pieces and align them
5. **clean finish sew** sides, leaving 2 inch (5cm) slits on either side at bottom
6. fold over top edge 1½ inches (3.8cm) and **flat hem** around waist for draw string
7. tie knot at 1 end of ribbon and **thread through** hem; **plain knot** at other end
8. tie corners in **simple knots** as shown

#60

ava

twisted hair
wrap

You'll need
1 large oblong scarf

1. drape scarf over your head with one side hanging down farther than the other as shown
2. cross scarf ends behind your neck
3. twist the longer end and place it around your head
4. tie it in place with a **simple knot** in back of head

#61

abbi

collar tie

You'll need
1 small square scarf
1 pin or brooch

1. fold scarf in half on the diagonal
2. place scarf around your neck as shown
3. make a **simple knot** in front with scarf ends
4. attach pin to scarf to add a little spice

#62

tula

top with appliqué

You'll need

1 polo type shirt

1 medium square scarf

1 medium oblong scarf

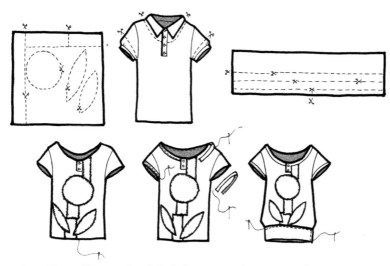

1. cut off collar of shirt to create u-neck
2. cut off sleeves to make cap sleeves
3. cut out shapes as indicated from square scarf; 1 circle, 2 leaves, and 3 strips
4. cut 4 2-inch (5cm) strips from oblong scarf
5. sew on shapes as shown using **zigzag** technique
6. using **border** technique sew long strips on sleeves and neckline to cover raw edges
7. sew remaining strip from oblong scarf around the bottom of the shirt, **gathering** slightly

63

alya

evening cover-up

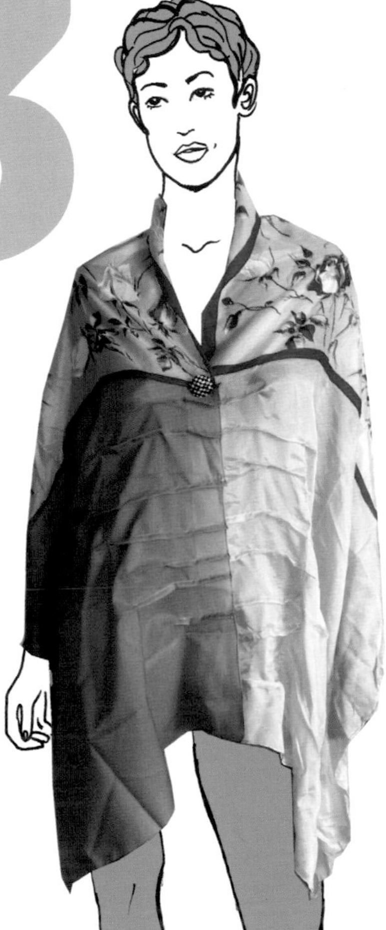

You'll need

2 medium square scarves

1 large square scarf

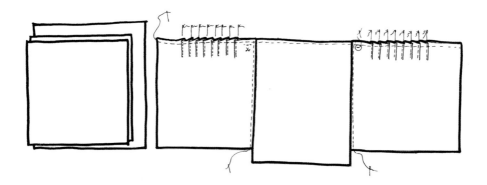

1. **clean finish sew** scarves together in a row with the large scarf in the center
2. sew 8 small **closed darts** into both medium scarves on top side as shown
3. make one **buttonhole** in inner corner of one medium scarf
4. **sew button** onto other medium scarf in corresponding corner
5. drape over shoulders with medium scarves hanging on either side in front
6. button to close

#64

antonella
poof-sleeve T

You'll need

1 medium rectangular scarf

1 fitted T-shirt or jersey top

1 foot (30.5cm) of elastic

sleeve shape

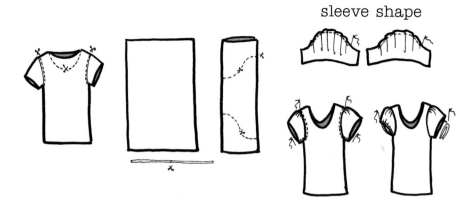

1. cut u-neck in back and front of T
2. cut off sleeves of T
3. fold scarf in half lengthwise
4. cut out sleeve shape using **pattern** technique
   [ATTN: be sure that length of long flat edge
   of sleeve shape is 2 inches (5cm) longer than
   circumference of armhole]
5. make **pleats** on curved side of sleeve shapes
6. **clean finish sew** sleeves onto armholes, making
   sure to close them under the arm as shown
7. cut elastic strip in half
8. **gather elastic** onto outer edge sleeve as trim

#65

camilla
v-neck tie top

You'll need
2 medium square scarves
1 large oblong scarf

1. fold both square scarves into triangles
2. tie ends into a **simple knot** as shown
3. drape scarves behind neck and over chest; adjust as desired
4. place oblong scarf around your waist and secure with **simple knot** or bow
   [ATTN: beware when dancing in this sexy top, you may end up showing off more than your dancing skills!]

66

kristen
scoop-neck
mini-dress

You'll need
1 tank top
1 extra-large rectangular scarf

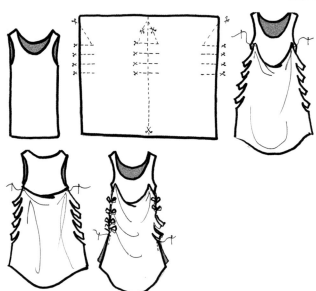

1. cut 16 slits in side and center of scarf where shown
2. cut scarf in half
3. **hand stitch** 1 scarf piece onto tank top in front with several stitches in corners [ATTN: make sure the slits are towards the top of tank top]
4. repeat with other piece on back
5. tie slits with **simple knots** on sides as shown
6. sew a few stitches onto either side beneath last knot for reinforcement

#67

allison
twisted-tie top

You'll need
1 medium square scarf
2 small square scarves

1. **simple knot** 2 corners of medium scarf to 2 corners of 1 small scarf
2. twist small scarf in front and tie it in a **simple knot** in back around neck
3. **roll** second small scarf
4. use a **simple knot** to tie it on both ends of bottom corners of medium scarf. oooh! you're so twisted!

#68

68

petra
placemat

You'll need

1 piece of plastic pvc thin enough to sew

1 medium rectangular cotton scarf

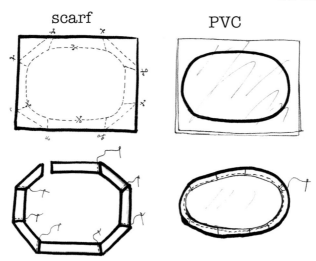

scarf

PVC

1. use an existing placemat as a stencil; placing it on top of your scarf, draw the outline of the placemat
2. use scarf remnants to make 1½ inch (3.8cm) wide strips
3. sew all of your strips into 1 long strip
4. place scarf between 2 pvc sheets, cut out same shape
5. fold strip around placemat, ¾ inch (2cm) on each side and sew using **border** technique
6. you have just made the cutest recycled placemat in world history; now make 5 more!!

69

carmela
bag bow

You'll need
1 small scarf
1 vintage purse

1. fold scarf in half on the diagonal
2. **roll** scarf
3. tie onto the strap of your favorite purse
   with a bow

#70

marlena

nifty neckpiece

You'll need
1 medium rectangular scarf

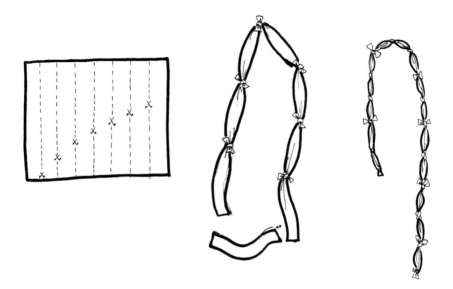

1. cut scarf widthwise into 1½ inch (3.8cm) wide strips
2. tie strips togther with **simple knots** into long nifty neckpiece
3. make several **plain knots** through out the piece for decoration
4. feel free to add charms at the bottom of the neckpiece for weight

#71

vania

arm warmers

You'll need

1 large square scarf

1 elastic strip 2 ft (61cm) long

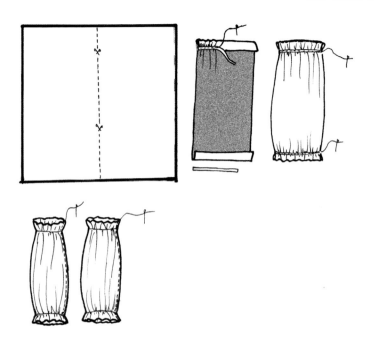

1. cut scarf in half
2. cut elastic strip in 4 equal pieces
3. take 1 scarf piece, fold both short edges down
   1½ inches (3.8 cm), and **gather with elastic**
4. fold piece in half lengthwise and **clean finish sew**
   long edges together
5. repeat for other arm warmer

#72

tori
flower pin

You'll need
1 small square scarf
flat cotton stuffing 4x4 inches
(10cm x 10cm)
large safety pin

1. find a scarf with big floral pattern (or if you dont have one, draw a flower on an existing scarf)
2. fold scarf in half with stuffing in between
3. **zigzag** stitch around the flower
4. cut flower out as shown
5. fasten safety pin on the back of flower with a few stitches (refer to illustration)

#73

mary
barrel bag

You'll need
1 large square scarf

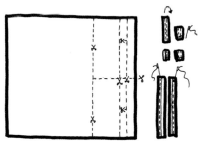

1. cut square scarf into two 1½ inch (3.8 cm) wide strips; cut one strip in half and cut the other into 4 even sized short strips; **flat hem** all strips
2. fold 4 short strips in half lengthwise and stitch closed creating 4 loops
3. cut a 6 inch (15cm) wide strip from scarf, then cut strip in half lengthwise
4. fold remaining scarf piece in half lengthwise, and **clean finish sew** the two 6 inch (15cm) wide strips onto sides as shown [ATTN: original hemmed edge of scarf must face upwards]
5. stitch 4 loops to top edge of bag where shown
6. thread 2 remaining strips through loop and stitch closed creating 2 shoulder straps. BRAVA!

#74

judith
shoulder tie tank

You'll need

2 large square scarves

1 large oblong scarf

0 sewing skills

1. place 2 square scarves on top of each other
2. tie upper corners together with **simple knots**
3. slip it on and tie oblong scarf around your waist
   with a bow or **simple knot**
4. you're done—and you are HOT!

#75

sierra

wrap around tank

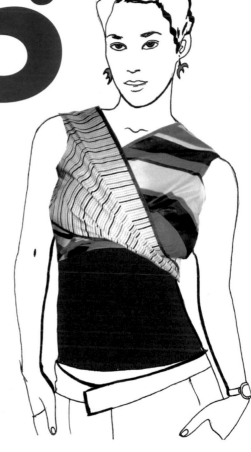

You'll need
2 large oblong scarves

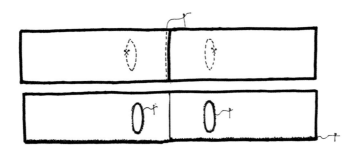

1. **clean finish sew** short sides of oblong scarves together to make 1 long scarf as shown
2. with new seam in back, calculate where you would like armholes to be; mark it
3. cut oval holes for armholes
4. **zigzag** stitch around armholes
5. slip on and cross two sides in front
6. tie in back with bow

#76

beverly

mini v-neck
t-shirt

You'll need
1 large square scarf

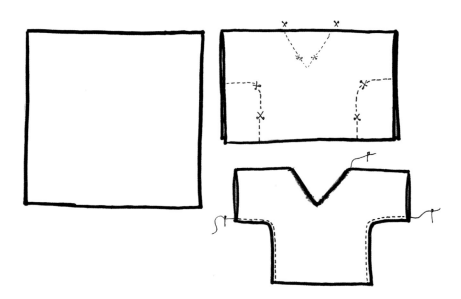

1. fold scarf in half
2. cut shape as indicated making sure armholes, head, and body openings correspond with your measurements
3. **clean finish sew** from bottom of mini t-shirt to armhole [ATTN: don't sew armholes shut!]
4. **zigzag** stitch around neckline

#77

marie

off-the-shoulder
mini-dress

You'll need
1 large square scarf
1 tank-top

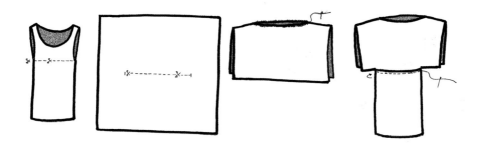

1. cut off tank top straight across underneath armholes
2. cut horizontal slit in center of scarf the same length as your measurements (shoulder to shoulder)
3. **zigzag** stitch around slit
4. fold scarf in half as shown
5. **zigzag** stitch tank to bottom of scarf, in center in front and back, leaving "armpits" open, as shown
6. time to boogie on down!

#78

alicia
bolero top

You'll need
1 large rectangular scarf

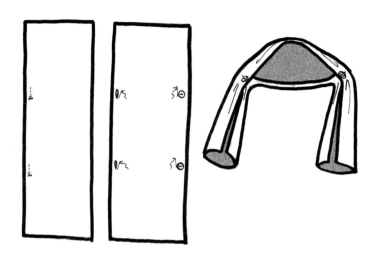

1. place scarf over shoulders and mark where you'd like the buttons to be under arms [ATTN: do not place buttons or buttonholes too close to edge of scarf]
2. make **buttonholes** on 1 long end of scarf, where indicated
3. sew 2 **buttons** on corresponding edge of scarf
4. drape over shoulders and button et voilá!

#79

agatha
ruffled collar

You'll need
1 medium oblong scarf

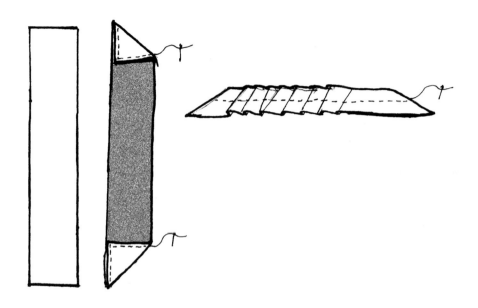

1. fold corners in and **top stitch** them down as shown
2. **pin and pleat** scarf and then sew all the way across the center of the pleated scarf to hold it in place, leaving 5–10 inches (12.5cm–25.5cm) of scarf for tying)
3. wrap around neck and tie with a **simple knot**

#80

carly
pretty top

You'll need

1 medium rectangular scarf

1 medium oblong scarf

1. cut and sew 4 **closed darts** into oblong scarf where indicated
2. **clean finish sew** rectangular scarf into large **tube**
3. **clean finish sew** oblong scarf closed by joining edges
4. **top stitch** oblong scarf onto scarf tube, **gathering** as needed in front and back as shown (make sure to leave space for armholes!)

#81

esther

tank with bows

You'll need

1 t-shirt

1 small square scarf

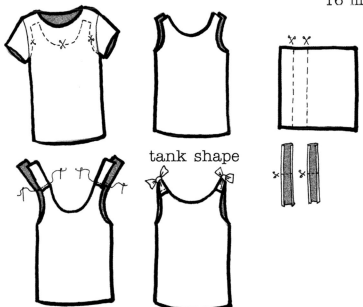

tank shape

1. cut out shape indicated from t-shirt to create tank shape
2. cut 2 strips from scarf 1 inch (2.5cm) wider than tank strap and at least 1 ft (30.5cm) long
3. cut strips in half and **flat hem**
4. **clean finish sew** the 4 strips onto tank—2 in front, 2 in back—as shown
5. tie strips as desired

#82

colette
lounge pants

You'll need

2 extra-large rectangular scarves

1 extra thin oblong scarf

1. cut both scarves in half as shown using **pattern technique** [ATTN: cutting indications for (a) and (b) are NOT identical]

2. **clean finish sew** pieces of scarf (a) together as indicated (in crotch) and repeat with scarf (b)

3. **clean finish sew** (a) and (b), front and back, to form pant legs (leave slits on bottom, outer side)

4. fold waist over 2 inches (5cm), and **roll hem** waist

5. **simple knot** bottom of pant on both legs as shown

6. cut 2 holes in front center of pants, 2 inches (5cm) apart

7. **thread** scarf (c) through draw string waist

8. **simple knot** scarf (c) at ends—several knots at an inch (2.5cm) or 2 apart is very cute

#83

iris

hat tie

You'll need
1 medium square scarf
1 wide-brimmed hat

1. fold scarf in half on the diagonal
2. **roll**
3. wrap around hat as shown and tie in place with
   a **simple knot**
4. secure scarf to hat with several **hand stitches**

84

rania
curtain

You'll need
6 square scarves
(size and quantity will vary depending on window dimensions)
curtain rod
clip-on curtain rings

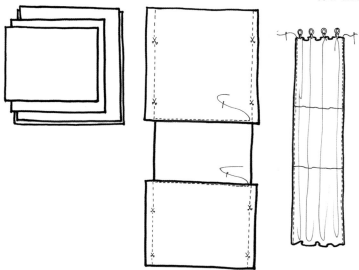

1. place scarves side by side in the order and direction you would like them to hang in the window, and pin together
2. **clean finish sew** scarves together as shown
3. cut off strips on sides if necessary to even them out
4. **flat hem** long sides
5. attach evenly spaced ring clips onto 1 short end of curtain
6. slide rings onto rod and enjoy the shade!

#85

lilian

funky top

You'll need

2 large square scarves

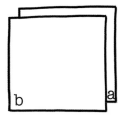
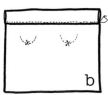
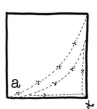

1. fold over 1 side of scarf (b) about 6 inches (15cm) and **roll hem**
2. place scarf (b) over shoulders to figure out where armholes need to be; mark them, then cut 1 "flap" on either side
3. cut scarf (a) in half diagonally, making a slight arch as shown
4. using smaller half (a), cut off an arched strip from longest side as indicated
5. cut hem from remaining piece that is about 1 inch (2.5cm) wide, then cut into 2 strips at corner
6. place large triangle from second scarf into front of top and **clean finish sew** onto both sides
7. hem strips around armholes using **border** technique
8. **thread** arched strip through collar, tie as desired

86

april
wide belt

You'll need
1 large oblong scarf
1 3 inch x 4 inch (7.5cm x 10cm) piece of cardboard

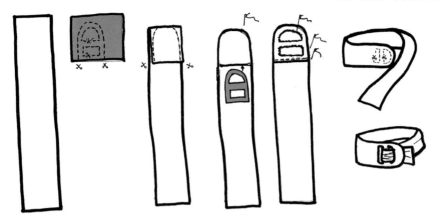

1. cut out belt buckle from cardboard (check out the shape in the drawing above for a guide)
2. fold over one end of scarf with wrong sides facing
3. insert buckle and use a pen to outline buckle on scarf adding ¼ inch (6mm) around
4. take out the cardboard buckle and sew around outlines as shown to make a "buckle pocket"
5. trim excess corners, then flip created "buckle pocket" inside out and put buckle back inside
6. cut holes in scarf for buckle holes
7. hand sew around edges to cover and secure your lovely cardboard buckle

#87

luna

macrame
halter top

You'll need
1 tank top
1 medium square scarf

1. cut off top of tank under armholes
2. cut scarf into 1½ inch (3.8cm) wide strips
3. **clean finish sew** 2 strips into 1 long strip
4. use **border** technique to sew long strip around raw edge of the tank

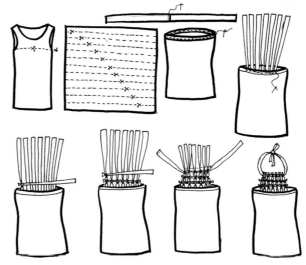

5. **hand stitch** 7 strips onto front of tank as shown
6. take 1 strip and **simple knot** it to first vertical strip 1 inch (2.5cm) above tank edge; then **simple knot** the same strip to 2nd strip, then 3rd, and continue knotting across all 7 strips
7. repeat with the next strip; then the 3rd and so on until all strips are used
8. cut off any dangling strip pieces
9. **simple knot** the 2 strips from the top corners of completed macrame, tie strips at back of neck

#88

dakota
high-waisted skirt

#89

mikael
asymmetrical strapless dress

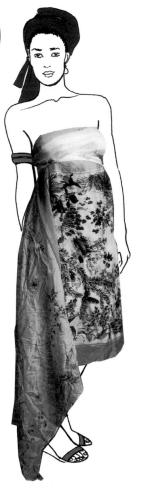

You'll need

1 large oblong scarf

2 large square scarves

1 large rectangular scarf

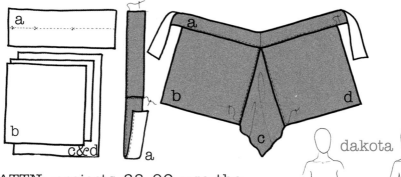

dakota

mikael

[ATTN: projects 88–90 use the same pattern; wear it 3 ways!]

1. cut (a) in half lengthwise; **clean finish sew** short ends together to create 1 long strip
2. **flat hem** raw edge
3. **clean finish sew** scarves (b), (c), and (d) together with (d) in the middle as shown
4. **clean finish sew** long strip (a), centered onto scarves (b), (c), and (d)
5. FOR DAKOTA: wrap around waist twice and tie in a **simple knot** on the side
5. FOR MIKAEL: wrap around bust twice and tie in a **simple knot** on the side

#90

tigra

tie neck mini
dress

You'll need

1 large oblong scarf (a)

2 large square scarves (b), (c)

1 large rectangular scarf (d)

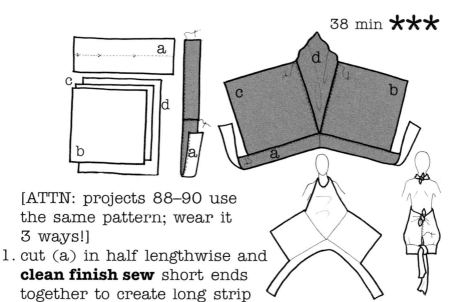

[ATTN: projects 88–90 use the same pattern; wear it 3 ways!]

1. cut (a) in half lengthwise and **clean finish sew** short ends together to create long strip
2. **flat hem** 1 raw edge
3. **clean finish sew** scarves (b), (c), and (d) together with (d) in the middle as shown
4. **clean finish sew** long strip (a), centered onto scarves (b), (c), and (d)
5. take dangling corner of scarf (d) and pinch each side of corner and tie around your neck as a halter
6. tie corners of (b) and (c) together in a **simple knot**
7. sew from tie in corners to about 5 inches (12.5cm) before bottom
8. tie strip (a) in back

#91

porter
ruffle-sleeve sweater

You'll need

1 medium square scarf

1 long-sleeved cardigan

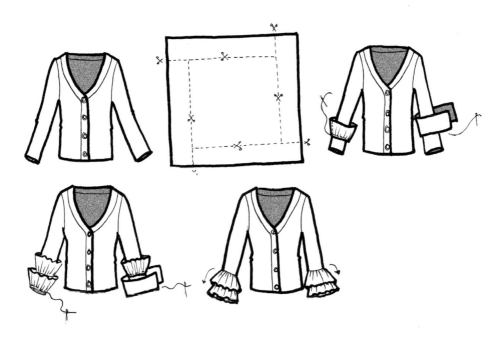

1. cut four 5 inch (12.5cm) wide strips from scarf as indicated
2. use **gathering** technique to sew 2 strips onto the inner edge of each sleeve
3. **clean finish sew** the ruffles' short edges together to close each ruffle

#92

beth

retro bow top

You'll need
2 medium square scarves

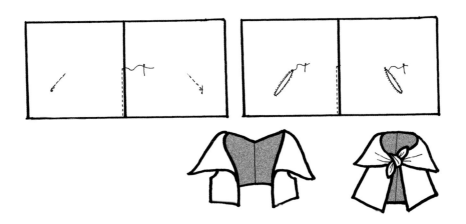

1. **clean finish sew** scarves together, leaving almost half unsewn as shown
2. place scarves over shoulders to figure out where armholes need to be, mark them, and cut 2 diagonal slits for armholes in center of both scarves where marked
3. **zigzag** stitch around armholes
4. fold big collar down and tie corners in front

#93

florence

pocket scarf

You'll need
1 large wool oblong scarf
(we recommend 1 with short fringe for
decoration)

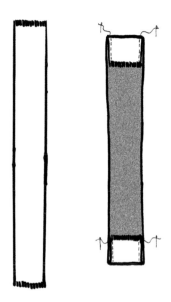

1. fold down ends of scarf 5 inches (12.5cm) each
2. **top stitch** long sides to create pockets as shown
3. feel free to decorate by stitching on a silk scarf patch as shown in picture

#94

toni

hippie bag

You'll need

1 medium oblong scarf

1 medium rectangular scarf

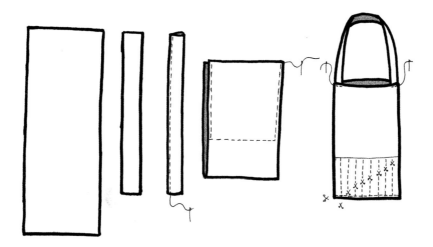

1. sew oblong scarf into **tube** lengthwise
2. fold rectangular scarf in half widthwise
3. **top stitch** down long sides of folded scarf stopping 8 inches (20.5cm) from bottom fold; stitch across to connect sides as shown
4. cut horizontal slits to create 2 layers of fringe
5. cut across bottom (folded) edge of fringes to double their number
6. stitch tube to upper corners of bag for shoulder strap

#95

marlena
poncho

You'll need

1 large square scarf

1 ribbon 2½ feet (76cm) long

1 pom-pom ribbon, long enough
to go around all edges of scarf

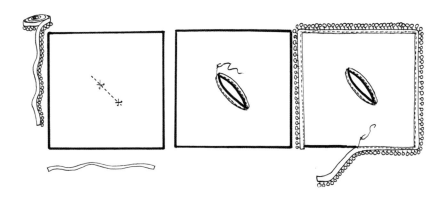

1. cut diagonal slit in center of scarf (be sure it's big enough to fit your head through)
2. use **covered hem** technique to sew ribbon around slit
3. **top stitch** pom-pom ribbon around edges of scarf for decoration
4. slip over your head and you're good to go!

#96

kimberly

beauty bag

You'll need
1 medium square scarf
1 vintage button

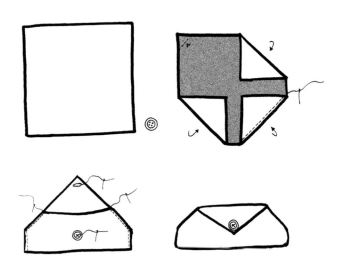

1. fold 3 of 4 corners toward center of scarf as shown
2. **top stitch** indicated edge
3. make **buttonhole** at folded corner
4. fold almost in half leaving corner with buttonhole for flap
5. **clean finish sew** sides closed where shown
6. sew **button** onto front in correspondence with buttonhole

#97

dietra

multi-scarf collar

You'll need
3 square scarves of
various sizes
1 chilly day

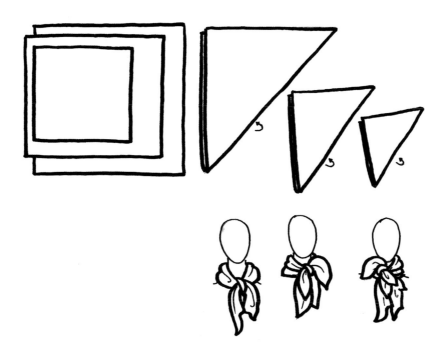

1. fold scarves in half on the diagonal
2. tie largest scarf around your neck
3. tie medium scarf around your neck
4. tie small scarf around your neck
5. now you're set for paris, bon voyage!

june

t-shirt dress

You'll need

1 extra-large rectangular scarf

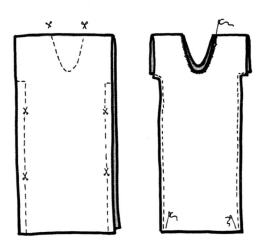

1. fold scarf in half lengthwise
2. cut out neckline as you wish (we chose a deep v-neck)
3. cut off strips from both sides on front and back [ATTN: the longer the strips the smaller the arm holes, the wider the strips the tighter the dress]
4. **clean finish sew** the sides closed as shown [ATTN: don't sew the armholes shut!]
5. **zigzag** stitch around neckline

#99

irina

victorian-style top

You'll need
2 large square scarves

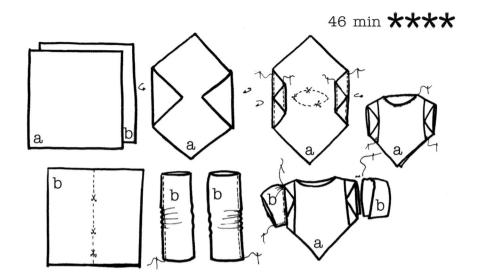

1. fold 2 opposite corners of scarf (a) toward center
2. fold these 2 corners of scarf (a) halfway back
3. **top stitch** folded edges lengthwise to secure folds
4. cut hole in center of scarf, **zigzag** stitch raw edge
5. fold scarf (a) in half at head hole as shown
6. **clean finish sew** sides beneath armholes
7. cut scarf (b) in half and sew into **tubes**, **gathering** slightly at center as shown (for puffiness)
8. **clean finish sew** tubes to armholes joining seam of tubes to folded armhole edge, gathering side up
9. **clean finish sew** sleeves together under arms

glossary techniques

pin before sewing

Pin fabric down **before sewing** to help keep fabric in place.

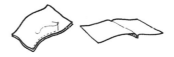

clean finish sewing

Sew fabric inside-out by putting the 'right' sides face to face; after sewing, turn right side out so that raw edges remain inside and unseen.

sewing on buttons by hand

Tie knot in thread. Push needle through fabric and button-hole. Repeat. Bring needle back up through fabric and wrap thread around the thread that is between fabric and **button.** Fasten with knot underneath fabric.

making buttonholes

Draw a line slightly larger than the diameter of button to be used. Zigzag stitch around dotted line (don't stitch over line). Make opening with sharp scissor between stitches.

glossary techniques

gathering

Fabric is **gathered** by making tiny folds in the fabric and sewing over the folds with small stitches. Unless otherwise indicated, **gather** fabric before sewing it onto desired location.

gathering with elastic

The piece of elastic should be about half the length of the fabric that will be **gathered** (when possible, try to measure the amount of **elastic** needed on your body). Pin the tip of the elastic onto the fabric, and stretch the elastic with your hand while sewing (using the zig-zag stitch) over the elastic and fabric.

glossary techniques

closed darts

To create **closed darts** pinch a triangle of fabric and sew the edges of the triangle together. Then iron flat in a downward direction.

open darts

To create an **open dart**, cut a triangle into the fabric and sew edges of the triangle together. Then iron remaining raw edges flat.

pin and pleat (inverted pleats)

Fold fabric into **pleats** (ironing folded edges can facilitate pleat-making) and pin the folds into place.

stuff/stuff and quilt

Evenly place soft filling on fabric. Lay second piece of fabric on top and sew all edges closed. If needed, sew small stitches over cotton for **quilted** effect.

glossary techniques

flat hem

To make a **flat hem**, fold edge upward and stitch flat.

rolled hem

To make **rolled hem** fold edge 2 times (raw edge should remain on the inside) then sew on top with top-stitch.

covered hem

To make **covered hem**, sew fabric strip on to raw edge with "right" side out. Then fold edge of strip upward while folding under raw edge of fabric; iron flat. Top-stich on the edge of fold.

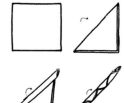

scarf roll

Fold square scarf in half on the diagonal; **roll** scarf from diagonal. Roll downward until scarf is completely rolled.

glossary techniques

top stitch

For **top stitch**, place fabric on top of other piece of fabric and stitch on top.

hand stitch

For **hand stitch**, sew by hand with doubled thread. Use stitch for thick layers or delicate sewing.

zigzag

For a **zigzag stitch**, sew around edges with the zigzag stitch on your sewing machine (also useful for stretch fabrics and elastics).

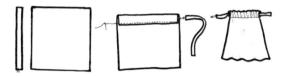

threading through

Roll hem edge of fabric leaving at least ½ inch (13mm) space in the fold; put a safety pin on edge of ribbon and stick it inside the hem, pushing the pin to **thread through** until it gets to the other opening (use for drawstrings).

glossary terminology

tube

from strip to band

from rectangle to tube

from "half-circle" to cone-like tube

from strip to long tube

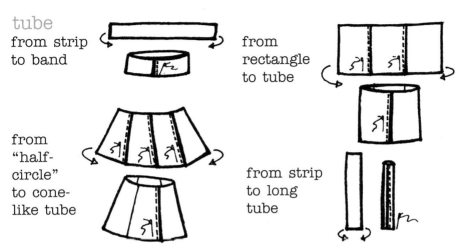

Clean finish sew all tubes unless otherwise indicated

simple knot

1   2   3   4

plain knot

glossary

pattern making technique for pants

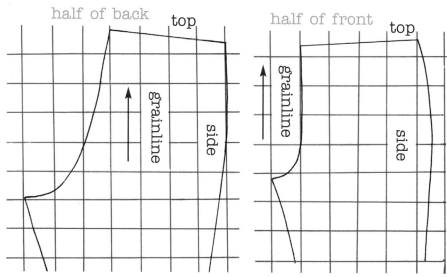

half of back

top

half of front

top

grainline

grainline

side

side

to adjust pattern size:
add or subtract ½ inch
(13mm) from side to
increase or decrease
size, from top to
increase or decrease
height of waist

*enlarge this pattern so
that each square in the
graph is equal to 2 inches
(5cm) x 2 inches (5cm).

Once enlarged on paper, create the full pattern including left
and right sides; pin sides and crotch together, then try on
paper pattern to ensure a good fit.

glossary

pattern making technique for bikini bottom

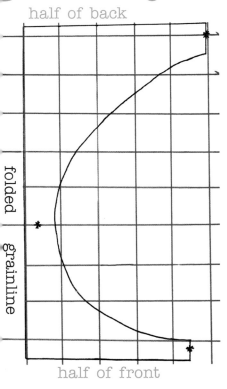

half of back

folded · grainline

half of front

*enlarge this pattern so that each
square in the graph is equal to
2 inches (5cm) x 2 inches (5cm).

create full pattern
add or subtract ½ inch (13mm)
where indicated with an asterisk
to increase or decrease size

*the pattern's crotch
length should be equal
to your body's crotch
length plus ½ inch
(13mm)

Once enlarged on paper, create the full pattern including left and
right sides; pin sides and crotch together, then try on paper pattern
to ensure a good fit.

glossary

pattern making technique for top

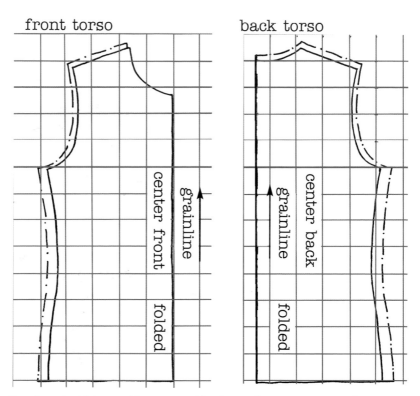

front torso

back torso

center front
grainline
folded

center back
grainline
folded

*enlarge this pattern so that each square in the graph is
equal to 2 inches (5cm) x 2 inches (5cm).

glossary

pattern making technique for sleeve

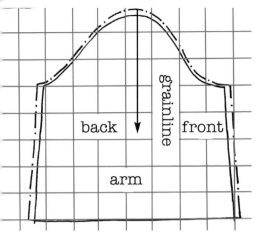

back | grainline | front

arm

*enlarge this pattern so that each square in the graph is equal to 2 inches (5cm) x 2 inches (5cm).

**for Antonella #64 enlarge this pattern so that each square in the graph is equal to 3 inches (7.5cm) x 3 inches (7.5cm)

se these patterns for neck lines, sides, shoulders, arm holes nd sleeves. Feel free to adjust the sleeve holes and necklines or desired shapes. The innermost lines in the patterns are or a size small, the outermost lines are for a size large. For size medium, draw lines in between the innermost and utermost lines.

Once enlarged on paper, create the full pattern including eft and right sides and pin sides and shoulders together; try n paper pattern to ensure a good fit.

Once you're happy with the fit of the pattern, pin it to abric, and cut out pieces.

acknowledgments

OK. Here comes the part where we give a shout out to everyone who has contributed to the making of this epic trilogy. We'd like to start by thanking our creators; from the guru in the sky to the families (moms and pops always hookin' it up) that are our roots. We would like to thank the crew at Potter Craft with a special shout out to Rosy, Erin, Amy, Paige, and Isa. We would like to thank **Tina, Pam, Derek, and Rosy** for letting us use their scarves. To our agent **Melissa** (you rock!) and **Brad** and **Shia** for that connection. To **Caitlin, Bene, Sarit,** for advice, ideas, modeling, and babysitting. To Kimberly, for your skillz. To **VERA** for your endless creative inspiration.

Check us out at www.COMPAI.com to find out more about us, the haps, and our new clothing line and hit us up at compai.blogspot.com.